Selah

Pause and Reflect

Be Blessed

Psalm 91 v 1-2

Linda

Linda Daruvala

O&U
Onwards & Upwards

Onwards and Upwards Publishers
4 The Old Smithy
London Road
Rockbeare
EX5 2EA
United Kingdom
www.onwardsandupwards.org

First edition, published in the United Kingdom by Onwards and Upwards Publishers Ltd. (2020).

ISBN: 978-1-78815-610-3
Typeface: Sabon LT

To Jung, Pete and Simon

Seek out the 'Thin Places'
for there you will feel the touch of God

Endorsements

To write with simultaneous simplicity and depth is a skill which eludes many writers, yet Linda captures this beautifully in her poetry. Each poem invites us to pause, reflect and enter not just into the poem but into a holy moment - glimpsing the authentic moving relationship Linda has with Jesus. This gem of a collection invites, inspires and includes us all in glimpsing profoundly God's transformational love for each one of us every day.

Jennie Fytche
Training Provider, Mentor and Christian Schools Worker

I have always loved poetry in the same way I love art and music. It has the sublime power to linger in the mind and then move deep into the heart, and Linda's poems do just this. When I first met Linda, I was immediately aware of the inner peace that she carried. In my experience this can only be the wonderful result of knowing we are fully loved, and that comes from knowing God. And this peace, and love, come through her contemplative and gentle writing as she touches on the beauty of this world, the difficulties we face and the hopes we have. 'To a God I trust with my life' is one of my favourite lines. She asks us to trust, to reconnect and to be brave as 'God calls us out of the comfort zone'. Read on, take a poem a day at a time, and enjoy.

Jenny Hawke
Watercolour artist and author who loves seeing and interpreting expressions of faith through everyday life

Linda's poems are an inspirational aid to reflect and guide you into God's presence. A book to journey with on retreat or just sitting a while with the Lord. His awesomeness, beauty and presence can be sensed on each page. The relationship the writer has with the Beloved is tangible. It takes you through real experiences of life and expresses in words what our hearts at times cannot say. I can totally recommend this book as a companion to prayer and an aid to faith. What a Lord and Saviour we have.

Rev. Elizabeth Knifton
Associate Minister; Healing Advisor, Diocese of Guildford

Linda's poetry will help you slow down and see God weaving his presence in and through your everyday.

Rev. Dr. Russ Parker
Author of 'Wild Spirit of the Living God'

Nature and its beauty is a constant reminder of God's presence all around us, and these poems say this in different ways... The liminal boundary between heaven and earth is transparent...

Nonie Insall
Counsellor and Psychotherapist

About the Author

Linda grew up in Dorset, fell in love with poetry while studying Thomas Hardy's poems for O Level English and can still recite some of them! An only child, she has always found solitude a comfortable and creative space to inhabit. She gave her life to the Lord at 18 at teacher training college in Winchester, which is where she also began to write. A love of Jesus, travel, contemplation, quiet, photography and art all enable her to meditate and compose her poetry, reflections and prayers. She especially loves to retreat to 'thin' places throughout the UK, those areas of deep spiritual significance such as Iona, Holy Island and Wales. It was at Ffald y Brenin in 2019 that she felt a fresh call from the Lord into "creativity within the healing ministry".

Linda was a primary school teacher for many years in the UK and four years in Brunei where she met her husband Jung. They live in Surrey and are so proud of their two wonderful adult sons, Pete and Simon. Since being healed from Non Hodgkins Lymphoma in 2010, Linda has particularly relished every day and is a member of the prayer ministry team at Acorn Christian Healing Foundation. She is passionate to pray in Jesus' Name for others' healing in body, mind and spirit with a compassion that comes from the Lord's heart.

Linda has led a number of creative quiet days to encourage others to express their faith-life in art and crafts. She has herself been inspired by the creativity within many Christian retreat centres, in Ignatian spirituality and new Celtic monasticism. Linda delights to sing in her church worship band and her joy is to spend time at a little rented beach hut on Hayling Island. She loves listening to God, new travels, sunsets, watercolours and Jung's delicious beef stroganoff.

Thank you:

Dear Father God, Lord Jesus and Holy Spirit for loving, guiding and inspiring me.

Jung, Pete and Simon for always letting me be me.

Many companions alongside me on the journey of faith. Many friends who have encouraged me to publish – well, here it is!

And, of course, Luke and his publishing team for liking my poems.

Contents

Foreword by Rev. Wes Sutton

Sometimes the gifts God brings into your life are people, and Linda Daruvala is one of them. She has met Jesus the Healer (but that is her story to tell, not mine) and it has left an indelible imprint on her life and in her poetry.

Selah is not simply a collection of poems, it is the expression of a life lived closer to God than might often be the case in our modern church or world. As I read these gemstones of God's grace, I felt the breath of the One who inspired them. Linda would not lay claim to be a theologian, but she brings to us a 'living theology' to illustrate the heart of God and inspire within us a hope and trust in Him.

Although each poem can be read individually, I would encourage you to read the five poems centred around Passion Week as one thing. 'Sounds in the Night' took me to Gethsemane. 'Malchus' – wow! – it left me holding my breath; I felt I was standing next to him – that close to Jesus. 'Peter's sandals', 'The Nails' and 'The blood of the Lamb' mean that Easter will not be the same again for me.

Linda writes with an astute perception of our humanity and our spirituality. 'Paparazzi' and 'Lone Jogger' (until you stop running) and 'Greater Than >' are reflections on life and us, that make you look in the mirror of poetry and see yourself a little more clearly. 'Carols at Christmas' just left me stunned with the realisation, to quote the work of Brennan Manning, that even after all this time "I am still being converted to Christ".

As someone involved in the healing ministry of Jesus, can I say that 'The Healing of the Blind Man' could only come from the pen of someone who has stood where Bartimaeus stood and received what Bartimaeus received.

If you let Linda's gentle words into your life you will find Jesus not too far away, and like me, you will find yourself returning to this book again and again. So note this; you are holding a classic in your hands, even now.

Rev. Wes Sutton
Director, Acorn Christian Healing Foundation

Diamonds on the Soles of His Shoes

Jesus passed this way today:
The frosted ground sprinkled with iridescent diamonds,
Sparkling rainbow drops suspended from each grass blade,
Scattering of Swarovski crystals abound.
Sunbeams become spotlights on ethereal colours,
Tiny lights of azure, amber, jade and topaz –
Just frozen water droplets in the presence of the Light…
Such beauty that captivates our eyes.
Yes, Jesus walked through this garden today
And as He journeyed,
Diamonds dropped from the soles of His shoes
And left imprints to delight, fascinate and still us.
Just to let us know
That He, God, passed this way
And He leaves His gift to us.

Note: I had arrived early at Whitehill Chase and I took a photo of a lawn which was covered with frost, just beginning to melt in the bright morning sun. And as it was melting, glittering rainbow colours shone through the droplets creating a dazzling sight.

Contemplation

Raw
Simple
No embellishments
In the quiet, alone.
Time pauses.
One to one, eye to eye,
Mind to mind, heart to heart.
Vulnerable, open, real, exposed
To a God I trust with my life.
To speak, to seek, to lift, to despair,
To cry, to pray, to understand, to ask,
To learn, to encounter, to find peace,
To breathe, to feed, to drink, to satisfy,
To acknowledge, to appreciate, to magnify.
Time alone,
Well spent.

Wild Winter Wind

Fresh cool invigorating wind on my cheeks.
Black trees silhouetted as if burnt against a grey smoky sky;
Each one responding differently to the Wild Winter Wind.
The silver birch gracefully dangles its delicate feathery fronds
That waft like palms in a summer Caribbean breeze;
A ballerina beauty, a rhythmic ebb and flow like the tide.
The bright green conifer jauntily bouncing
Like a jolly fat policeman laughing heartily.
The blossomless cherry tree shudders as one –
A sudden shiver, then is at peace again.
The tiny snowdrops beneath nod at each breath,
Like opaque water droplets on the brink of falling,
Freshwater pearls amidst soft jade.
The evergreen rhododendrons dance a merry jig
Battering each other's buds with a carefree flamboyance.
New elegantly tall daffodil leaves slap and flap happily
    together,
Relieved that as yet they have no new buds to protect.
The dry leaves caught up in a gusty whirlwind swirl and
    scatter,
Tumble and fall, like children in a playground.
Strong sturdy shrubs wiggle tentatively, bracing themselves
For the next momentary blast.
Holy Spirit of God, Ruach, Wild Wind of God
Blows where He pleases, we do not control Him,
But we know where He is.

May I respond to You in the way I am created.
May I yield and bend, dance or sway, laugh or nod.
As Your breath blows on us all, we respond as we are.

Withdrawal

Lord, out of my comfort zone
Is engaging when preferring to be alone.
I am sure Christ felt the same
Preferring quiet, lonely places in isolation
To connect and reconnect with You.
Yet most times He was found,
His secret places discovered, and He turned
To face humanity yet again, touching,
Reaching out, healing, explaining.
This is Your Will, His purpose,
Although He craves intimacy, His hands
And words reveal You, O God.
No other name, no other person
Can reveal as He is to You.
Enable me to recognise those moments
When I would withdraw and separate from society
Which is good and pleasing to You
But of so much more gain if I share
People's journeys and listen and pray.
It is my choice – thank you for the unease
I feel when I have made the wrong decision
And taken the easy path, not Yours.

In the Spotlight

Caught in the spotlight
So bright
Beaming from afar
Illuminates me
No hiding place
Captured in a brilliant dazzling aurora
I cannot see
But others view me
Stagestruck
Immobilised
As the Father's light envelops me, He
Pierces the darkness I would conceal
Reveals the shallowness of my love
And my limited understanding of who I am –
Who I am in Christ...
I am in Christ
And He is in me
As the light burns deeper into my soul
He opens an ever-deepening intimacy
A closer friendship
A wiser relationship
A cleaner venue
More of Jesus within me
And more of me in Him
Lord, flood my soul with your light
Illuminate the eyes of my imagination

That I may see, feel, hear, touch and taste Your Presence
Deeper and clearer than ever before
Throughout this year
My Lord and My Saviour
Amen.

Note: Based on Ephesians 1 v.18

Lockdown Easter 2020

It's just a Pause
Not an End
Nor a Beginning
Rather an Advent
An expectation of Something New to Come.

Creation breathes freely
Unhindered by polluted air
Or ravaged by consuming humans.

We find Time again;
Choices on what to do, who to contact.
Friends to cheer up or commiserate with,
Neighbours to befriend with a two-metre wave.

Banging Thursday saucepans relieves frustrations
And applauds our keyworkers,
Lives placed on the frontline.

Jesus is our Frontline Keyworker,
Had no PPE, no mask or sanitiser,
No political directives yet heavenly objectives.
An urge to go forward, self-isolate on the Cross,
To relinquish mankind from their bonds and chains
To set them free.

Is He doing it again,
This Easter?

When R is a number

I remember when
My mother would unpick an old hand-knit jumper
To reuse the wool.
Nimble fingers winding round and round,
Wrapping the wrinkled fibres into a tight ball
Of knotted harsh threads.
It looked uneven, worn out, tatty,
But it was the days of 'make do and mend'
For a school sweater, winter gloves, father's socks.

Easing of lockdown feels like this –
Original complete closure unravelling in a crinkled mess.
Ambiguous proposals mixed with negativity,
Rebellion and fear,
Anger and ignorance,
Speed and pressure,
Confusion and frustration,
Predictions and disagreements,
Demands and backtrack,
Media shame and attack.

"We've had enough," they say
"Why...?"
"How...?"
"When...?"
"We want our life back:

Barbecues, shopping, childcare, holidays...
Wage packets, dentists, foodbanks, funerals..."

Community obedience soon turned to anarchy,
A cohesive kindred spirit back to selfishness.
Faded child-painted rainbows.
We held something so precious
And have we sullied it, rejected it, discarded it
All too easily?

Forgive us, Lord.

Note: We have watched the constant daily updates of the 'R' number throughout this time of coronavirus. (The R number represents the average number of people an infected person goes on to infect.)

It was based on the media coverage of crowded, litter-strewn beaches, newspaper headlines and the disagreements between politicians, scientists and educationalists.

Coronavirus Shopping

The Brits are good at queueing, so it comes as no surprise
To leave two-metre distance, to pass and stand aside.
Measured out like soldiers, masked, on full alert,
Folded arms, watching phones, so nobody gets hurt.
Assistant smiles and waves them in, trolleys sprayed ahead,
Everyone obedient against the virus dread.
"Don't touch the rail!" the mother cries, plastic gloves put on.
Moving ants along a trail; where has it all gone wrong?
Face masks a fashion statement – spotted, patterned, plain –
Oh, when will our supermarkets be as they were again?
Invisible magnetic force repels people away,
Lives downtrodden, mouths downturned; let's just get through
    this day...
Sanitising gel squeezed out, "Keep a safe distance" tops
Entrance this way, exit that; the same for all our shops.
Covid-19, what have you done? We're feeling all forlorn –
Can't browse the shelves or try things on, be so glad when
    you've gorn!

Gratitude

Father,
Thank you that You are Almighty God;
For You created the earth in all its beauty
From iridescent damselfly and fragile swallowtails to
Majestic cedars, mighty ocean, starlit skies,
Faint cuckoo call to elephant's trump,
Cool black of night to hot glare of day,
Spiny thorns prick to smooth velvet of cat,
Sweet flesh of peach to warm coconut milk.

Thank you for human thought, emotions and love,
The ability to worship You and
Express delight and adoration with all our being.
Thank you that You have reserved a place for me
In Your kingdom, both on earth and in the heavenlies,
For angels to protect and guard me.

But Father, pain penetrated your heart
When you surrendered your son Jesus
For my life.
Such sacrificial love, Father – how do I 'thank you' for that?
I cannot do enough to repay my debt,
Except to say that
I love you and offer you my life.

Come into my life, Holy Spirit, and

Change me, renew me, mould me, refresh me
To be a living channel for Almighty God
To honour his worthy name.
Amen.

Hayling Island – Watching Jet Skis

Riot of vivid colour, movement, fun –
Powerful jet skis breaking the surf,
Speeding and muscular.
Glistening, skimming, spraying, exhilarating,
Splashing, leaping, conquering the waves.
Manoeuvring like dodgems.
Cutting across white crests, bouncing, revving,
Heading from the safety of the bordered inlet
Out to the unlimited channel.

God calls us out of the comfort zone
With our gifting and excitement
Into unknown areas no eye can see.
Venture into the distance.
Seek the greater vision.
The horizon beckons
A far grander and wider
Yet more dangerous experience.
Be brave.

The Latch

Today, Lord, You have searched my heart
In a place I didn't expect You to uncover.
But Your thoughts entered my mind
So clearly and with such perfect timing.
I came with expectations of
Coming 'home' in other areas.
But You know me better than I know myself,
And You gently laid Your finger
Upon that latch, and said,
"Let's open this door and let Me in,"
And You have done so.

Sounds in the Night

All was quiet
Maybe distant merriment in Jerusalem of people greeting late
   arrivals for Passover
Lights twinkling in the homes
Donkeys' hooves on cobbled streets

But here in Gethsemane
Just the scrape of sandalled feet on well-worn paths
Not a word
Shuffling clothing snagged by shadowed thorns
A gentle cool breeze swaying the drooping silver olive branches
Leaves brushing against each other tenderly – *sssh sssh sssh*
Murmur of Jesus at prayer accompanied by heavy breathing
   and snores
Sighs of exhaustion
Silent tears

Harsh voices approaching
Shouts, clamour, stamping, clash of steel, crackling torches
In pursuit of vengeance
Mob rule

But then did all noise and commotion instantly cease, did wind
   still,
Did all heaven pause to hear the sound of
A moist kiss?

Did that sound reverberate on Christ's cheek, shudder his
heart, tremble his body?
Did it echo throughout the garden, whispered from tree to
tree?
Did the very soil groan and guardian angels cease to sing?
Did the gnarled trees creak and stoop to protect Him?

The betrayer's kiss
Followed by one word, softly spoken through deceitful lips –
Rabboni

Malchus

I have heard we arrest the blasphemer tonight
In some olive grove outside the city
Away from the crowds
Those uncouth followers might be with him
But they'll be no trouble
Easily frightened and scattered
At last, the one who has infuriated our high priest
Led the people astray
Insulted our religious leaders,
Discarded our historical laws
Sought people to follow him instead of Jehovah
Disrupted temple worship
Threatened the Roman government
Did magical illusions
Ate with brazen prostitutes and sly tax collectors
Talked openly with women and dirty gentiles
Deceived poor slaves into thinking they are important.

Tonight is the plan
We have inside information exactly where he will be.

It's very late
Lit by flaming torches
Faces set like the steel of our swords
We march uphill
At first stealthily then animated

To capture this so-called king.
Then a pause
We stand still, expectant
Something happening ahead
I am ushered forward and move through the throng of ruffians
I am quite close to this Jesus now
I see another greet him with a kiss
This is the signal
We have him!

Then shouts and clamour
Bit of a fight
I feel a sharp slice down the side of my face
Everything is muffled
I collapse in searing pain
I place my hand against the gaping wound
I touch sticky blood and cannot feel my ear
Everything continues around me
No one notices me.
I feel faint, my head swimming
My cries for help go unheard
Until I feel pressure on the wound
Heat and comfort
Something has happened.
I feel an ear again, full, complete, tender and smooth
Relief of agony
I hear clearly the words, "He who lives by the sword dies by
    the sword"
I look up into the face of this Jesus
Gentle, sorrowful piercing eyes

Reflecting the violence around him
An enigmatic smile
A personal miracle for me, Malchus

At this time of arrest, I'm so confused yet under orders
"Take me, let these others go"
We surround him
I continue to push him along with the crowd
But I am dumb
I cannot cry out harsh words of accusation
I keep feeling my ear
I am amazed
Did that really happen?
Is this Jesus the healer, the teacher, the actual Messiah?

Have we made a mistake?

Peter's Sandals

Not me, Lord!
My sandals are leather-worn
My feet dirty and soiled.
Yet I have to submit
To your compassionate yet authoritative eyes
That command me to let you
Undo the tough straps
Release the rusty buckle.
I feel ashamed, yet not humiliated.
What is it that you do, Lord?

You lift the grubby handle of the familiar old pitcher, servant's
    vessel,
And begin to pour the clear
Flow of water into the wooden bowl.
The water trickles,
All is silent.
Creation pauses
Not one speaks
All attention focussed on you, Lord
What is it that you do?

You take my feet and wash them gently, wiping
Soil and grime and sweat and dirt.
You remove the towel from your waist
Gently wipe my toes and sole and heel till

They feel cool and fresh in the air.
Such softness, wiping my feet
Tenderly smoothing until they are completely dry.
What is it that you do, Lord?

You undo more than my sandals, Lord
You undo my heart, and perplex my mind.
You not only clean my feet
You cleanse my soul
You not only dry my feet
But you dry my tears.
My mind in turmoil yet at peace
My heart overwhelmed by grace
My soul cleansed of shame and guilt
My spirit set free.
What is it that you do, Lord?

You demonstrate servanthood and say,
"Now go do thou likewise."

The Nails

The long, rusty nails, scarred, discarded from a previous task
Not easy to harshly hammer into flesh
No smoothness or fit for purpose
Strong, blunted, unyielding
Six inches of inflicted pain and torture
Staining, sinking, piercing, penetrating
Separating sinew and skin, tendon and bone
Driving relentlessly towards the thud of wood
Firmly grasping the King of Kings by the joints
Blood trickling, seeping, dripping
Searing pain, overwhelming, unbearable
Eyes close, flinch, agony
No escape now
No release now
Endured
For me

The Blood of the Lamb

The blood of the Lamb
Poured out from the heart of God
From the depths of his being
Wrenched out in pain and anguish.
God sacrificing himself for me,
Hung cursed on a tree
To let me live
In relationship with him.

What God of love is this?
To serve his own punishment
That I may go free?

Lord, there is something so deep here,
Almost too fragile and invaluable
To dare to touch its meaning and depth.
Yet as we draw near
To the power of the blood
So our condemnation is released
To walk in freedom and forgiveness.
One sacrifice, abhorrent and brutal,
Yet destructive to sin and
Complete in its simplicity.

Jesus Christ, Son of God,
I acknowledge the blood that you poured out for me

That my sins may be forgiven
And I may be blessed by the Lord my God
In health, joy, wisdom,
Righteousness, holiness and love.
Amen.

Paparazzi

They'd lost interest after that –
It had been phenomenal!
Sold front page headlines:
Chaos in the temple, challenging authorities, drinking with
    prostitutes,
Violent demonstrations, sordid allegations,
Polluted vox pop statements,
Secretive midnight fracas with weapons.

Intruded my Gethsemane, invaded my tears.
Hounded by their bellowing questioning,
500mm lenses aimed at my mournful eyes,
And still the automatic fire of flashguns focussed on my agony.
Dictaphoned my final words.

Just this limp bloodied figure on a cross...
All too common a sight,
Not newsworthy.

They've gone now, as has My Spirit.
I go to My Father,
But where do they go?
To the next uprising, zealot, apostle?
They crawl within Eden,
A feeding frenzy to shock and entertain.

But just who is the victim here?

Water from the Well

A dark pool of beautiful midnight-blue water...

You need to drink, drink deeply
The water is cool and clear
Pure and refreshing
It is life to you
Drink, and drink again to your fill
Enjoy the taste of the coolness on your lips
And the feel of the freshness down your throat
Calming the heat of your body
And revitalising your energy.

Cup your hands and drink
Lift your cup and drink
It is always flowing, everlasting
There in plenty and freely flowing
Always fresh and clean and pure
Every time you drink.

Enjoy the clarity, the taste, the feel
The abundance of dark, cool fresh water

Drink deeply, child, and keep drinking.

Lone Jogger

Lone jogger
With headphones
Shutting out the voice of the sea,
Casting a brief glance
At the beach.
Don't stop to reflect,
Press on to keep fit,
Got to keep going.
Listen to your blinding music,
Controlled by your Fitbit
To pursue your own goal.
You shut out God's call on you;
You won't hear Him or see Him
Until you stop running.

Conversation in the Poustinia

It's warm, pleasant to amble through wet grass
To the poustinia, turn the sign to "In Use",
Close a creaky door and settle into silence
Into a temporary cell with colourful crochet-covered chairs.
A candle gently lit, a steady flame.
Watching movements of the branches, hurried flitting of
    hidden birds.
Taupe twigs exploding with lime green leaf,
Beautiful bird chirruping accompanies the intense silence.
The sky transitioning from overcast smoky grey
To the promise of white streaks and gaps of blue.
All is still in my heart, yet the occasional rumble of a tractor
Or gardener's plastic pail murmurs in the background.
A pheasant calls, seagulls wail, crows caw.
A new gate leads onward to a newly ploughed field
Upturned ready for sowing – do I enter that gate
Into rough territory?

Child, you are blessed
I lay my kingdom before you
As an outstretched field
And I invite you to enter.
Yes, it may be virgin territory
But it is ploughed ready for service.
The difficulties have been surmounted,
Dark brought into light,

Good rich soil brought to the surface,
Fertile earth in which to sow seed,
A time to plant.

With what shall I plant?

Kingdom values of love, grace and compassion,
Justice for all, safe harbour and hermitage,
Community and isolation,
Comfort and solace, a seeking and a finding,
Health and wholeness.
Let me bless you with all you need for the task ahead.
Do you accept it?

Yes, Lord, I do. Show me your way and within it.
Show me your ways. Less of me, Lord, more of you.
I choose and I decide to follow You into the field,
Over the edge – you push and I will fly.
Let nothing distract or hold me back.

(At this point a wasp comes in...)

The wasp irritates, annoys, disrupts, creates fear.
Silence the wasps in my life, Lord.

I enter in, and am "In Use".

*Note: A poustinia (Russian) is a small, sparsely furnished cabin
or room where one goes to pray and fast alone in the presence
of God. This particular poustinia is in the grounds of the*

Northumbria Community, Nether Springs, Acton Home Farm, Felton, Northumberland.

We Sat on a Bench;
Salisbury Cathedral

We sat on a smooth wooden bench, engraved
"In happy memory, Pippa Nicholson, 1940-1989"
Facing a vista of green,
Looking up at magnificent majestic stonework.
To remember our friendship thus,
To sit awhile and contemplate
Happy memories.
Of laughter, tales of keys lost
And memorable quad biking trips.
Of floodlit plays within mediaeval walls.
Of gentle rain alongside the Mill Race.
Gazing at the elegance of cathedral's spire,
Prayer and fellowship together in a Christian home.
Happy memories
Of two souls finding out more about each other's
Life experiences
Hopes and dreams
Disappointments and adventures
Of future prospects and divine guidance.
Happy memories
Of the late Pippa and her friend
Of Rosemary and me.

West Face, Salisbury Cathedral

The eye wanders in wonder and awe
At each carved detail
Moving from deeply etched arch
To upright pillar
And sculptured portals.
How many statues? Maybe sixty
Clothed in drapes and robes,
Saintly bishops or mediaeval pilgrims
Remembered in stone.
But then
Beautiful floral-outlined windows,
Painstakingly carved details.
Yet the spire stands serene,
Unadorned with statues of personages,
Plain brick with a patterned motif and
At its peak, the cross.

A symbol, perhaps, of our religious journey:
At its beginning, full of people and decoration
Of ornaments and tradition and finery.
Yet as we draw nearer to God
These embellishments fall aside
And we adhere to the simplicity of God's Word
And the Cross.

Greater Than >

What sets me free?
His mercy is greater than my sin
His love is greater than my desire
His grace is greater than my weakness
His power is greater than my need
His peace is greater then my pain
His Word is greater than my flawed wisdom

I am loved even when my life is unlovely
I am safe whatever happens
I am not alone even if it feels like it
I am not forgotten because
God knows my name
I know there is a plan
Even though life seems random
I know that He is and *I am*

Market Day

Got to buy – it's cheap!
Cushions for our sofa
Jewellery for my neck
Clean your glasses? It's free
This will make your home look better
This will make you look better
This will improve your lifestyle.
You've always wanted one of those
T shirts hung in rainbow rows
Dare you pick up the XL?
Jeans, rude slogans, mobile phones,
Country music blaring, tattooed stall holders,
Fake Chinese rugs with false hessian backing.
Never mind, it's cheap.

For a few moments' pleasure
Your money is gone.
What have you of value?
Search for the precious things –
A pearl of great price.

Holy Spirit Like the Waves

Gentle but constant,
Soothing yet incessant,
Come Holy Spirit.
Ordained before time
To minister to men in need:
To bring refreshing in drought,
To bring warmth in shade,
To bring peace in adversity.
Quietly flowing in and through,
Relaxing, restoring, bathing,
Slowing, deepening, searching, scouring.
Have Your way.

Healing of Sight

Helpless, blind, stumbling and frail
Dependent, vulnerable, confused, perplexed
Coming towards Christ on hearsay.
He hears His voice, turns and seeks
The touch and words of sight.
He senses the closeness of the Master's robe
He feels the strength of palms on his face
Is still;
Hopeful beyond belief.
Thumbs press with authority into the sockets of
Opaque vision, tired, dismissed as useless.

A warmth, a light, a joy of the
Presence of God
Flowing through him,
Flooding his mind, his heart, his body.
New life springs up from within.
His heartbeat grows louder, resonates like a drum.
He cannot withhold his excitement
His eyelids fly open
"I can see!"

Colours, images, faces
He closes them in surprise
Is it a dream?
Cautiously opens them again, slowly

Firstly one then the other.
Focuses on the Face before him
The smile and loving eyes of his Healer
Jesus Christ.

What joy, gratitude, redemption, release
Expectation, hope, renewal.

Lord, may those who have been blinded
Be released in their sight
To the glory of Your Name
Amen.

Maundy Thursday

Lord Jesus
You wash my feet
Not for any agenda
Not to teach me something
Not to reveal yourself
But because it is
An immediate action
That comes from Your heart
And cannot be stilled;
An overpowering act of love
That needs to be.

May Dance

God gives us our ribbon
Long and free;
We take hold and begin to dance,
Interweaving with gaiety and rhythm.
Sometimes gloriously fast-paced
Twirling and lifting, carefree and resolute.
Other times pausing and bowing, retracing our steps
Letting others take the dance onward.
Laughter and silent apologies as we bump into an unsuspecting
    partner
Which knocks us slightly off track.

The colours merge and pattern,
Headdresses of blossom and bell
Jiggle along to the merriment.

Lord, may we interweave our lives
Among others, creating beauty and joy
To delight ourselves and those we meet.
But most of all, to make you smile.

May we, Lord, replace your crown of thorns
With a garland of spring flowers
For you, our Lord of the dance.

Spa Day

The sun sets quietly, gently
Over soft cream cushioned sunbeds.
Bubbling incessant jacuzzi as a waterfall
Cascading over a rock ledge.
Rippling swimming pool, warm blue inviting.
Clay terracotta pots of vivid red geraniums and variegated ivy
Perfectly placed, perfectly pruned.
Huge banana palms of the tropics,
And linen sunshades.
A hazy sky, scratched with glowing embers.
Perusing my cool exposed feet
As I still simmer from the treatments.
Everyone has gone.
There is tranquillity of body
And soul.

Baptism

Line of nervous candidates
Knowing God has brought them
To this moment in time
Standing aware of all eyes
Focussed on them
Of their witness to the church
And their unbelieving families
Different paths traversed
To converge at this time at this place
For God

Last minute fears
Stumbling over words of emotional testimony
But radiant smiles of faith
And security and expectancy in God
That this is their time
Whether aged nine or forty-nine

Crossed arms and a trust in the strength
Of the Pastor's arms around them
Moreover in the Father's arms around them
"I baptise you in the name of the Father, the Son and the Holy
    Spirit, Amen"
A splash
A moment's disappearance in the warm swirling depths
Applause

Soaked; immersed; uplifted

Some wipe the waters away
To regain their composure
Some eyes remain closed
Some heads bow in humility
Some stare ahead to ingrain the memory
Some leave water showering down their face and body
Revelling in its washing and freedom
Prolonging the profound experience
Of submission and submergence

Obedience is honoured today
All too briefly the moment passes
Like the "I do" of a marriage ceremony
Prophetic words spoken
Emotional verses from the Word
Individual pictures explained
A radical hope of a new future and a
Christ-directed vision

"Oh, taste and see that the Lord is good
All His ways are marvellous"

The Approach

I would but crawl and stoop...
But my Saviour urges me to look up,
To walk proudly and effortlessly towards Him.
No guilt or shame.
Forgiven, loved, welcomed,
Complete peace.
Angels silently blast their trumpets of joy,
Mists swirl and colours blend –
This is home.
Eternally.
Light radiating,
A golden crown placed on my head.
His child.
Your promise, guaranteed.

*Inspired by listening to the Asaph Music track 'Entering the
Throne Room'*[1].

---

[1] See http://www.asaphmusic.org.uk/anthems-of-ascent.html

Advent 2013

Do you see?
Did you see it?
Just there
Just a glimpse –
In the murky stench
And wailing of a newborn
Amongst the pungent dusty hay –
The gleam of a crown
Hanging down, suspended from the corner of an old manger
    trough.
A crown far too big for a baby
But ready to fit when His purpose is fulfilled
And He rises and returns to His throne room.

There – do you see?
Did you see it?
Just there
Just a glimpse –
Of ancient stones bathed in a purple shaft of light
As the sunrise pierces through the narrow opening
In a beam of glory and aurora glow
Colour of royalty.

The King is born
But yet, wait
His kingdom is yet to be.

"Behold," He says, "I am coming soon."

Look for Him –
Disregard the darkness of this world,
Strain your eyes and heart to see into the murkiness
And focus on the kingdom and the promise
For Immanuel has come
And touches us
With hope and life and eternity.

Advent 2015

Creating the door wreath today.

Wicker basket overflowing with fresh yew, ivy, spruce and
some red berries.

Twining stems tightly round the raffia base, pricked fingers as
I twist the holly.

Pause...

That crown of thorns, Lord, which adorned your bowed head,

Piercing pain of persecution.

I remember you.

A scented Yankee candle – Sparkling Snowfall – or some such
name.

A fresh scent powders the room,

The flickering wick wafting in the slight draught from the
window ledge.

Pause...

The Light of the World came into the darkness,

The darkness we continue to see

Of impetuous violence, radicalised youths, hidden abuse,
deceiving politicians,

Trudging migrants, grieving Parisians.

Shine, Jesus, shine Your light as this candle illumines my heart.

Coordinating beige reindeer gift tags, matching Nordic paper
and a wired silver bow,

Mitred corners and opaque tape carefully concealing Liz Earle
skin care gifts.

Pause...

I remember the boys wrapping with Woolworths' Santa
cartooned paper

A shoebox: packing toy cars, toothpaste and sweets for a "boy
aged 8-10"

Giving such surprise, joy and delight to an unknown recipient
in Kenya

That he might know love and generosity and ownership.

Placing the familiar nativity set on the marble mantelpiece, bit
dusty,

Kings on the right, shepherds on the left, kneeling Mary,
protective Joseph,

Baby's arms wide open with a cherub face, hand painted in
China.

Pause...

I don't think it quite happened like that, Lord,

Gold placed near manured straw reflecting the battered
manger,

An olive-skinned baby swaddled and soothed by a teenager,

Ointment jars, ornate and fragrant, nuzzled and toppled by
roving sheep,

Velvet, ermine, silk beside hessian and muslin, decadence
intertwined with poverty.

But there is a stillness, a reverence here that warms my heart
and causes me

To wonder in awe at the God who stoops to be born into my
world, into my life,

That I might know Him.

Lord, this Christmas time, amidst all the preparation of
   celebration
Please give me the grace and means and time to
Pause.

Newborn

Aaah, isn't he sweet?

Such beautiful eyes...
Such cute ears...
Chubby hands...
Tiny feet...
The sweetest breath...

...to see evil and injustice, tyranny and pain,
...to hear judgement and cursing, cries of woe and
   helplessness,
...to submit to betrayer, be harshly bound for trial,
...to walk the way of Calvary, emerge from the tomb,
...to proclaim freedom, to testify God's kingdom, to declare,
   "It is finished!"

Yes, He is sweet;
The sweet fragrance of Grace
Come down from heaven
That we might be
Sweet.

Carols at Christmas

What can I give Him,
Poor as I am? —
If I were a Shepherd
I would bring a lamb;
If I were a Wise Man
I would do my part, —
Yet what I can I give Him, —
Give my heart.

What can I give Him?
I come from a war-torn country
Ravaged by torture and injustice, persecution and torment.
My home is a burned-out shell, my children massacred.
I seek solace but all I hear are words of violence ringing in my
    ears.

What can I give Him?
I have been taught to fight for the cause
To rid the world of capitalism, to give my life
To be trained and prepared to kill and destroy.
To consider all the enemy, to hold my weapon close to my
    heart.

What can I give Him?
I am brought up by an alcoholic mother in poverty and dirt,
Known by the police, a truant and thief.

Fearful of the estate where I live, gangs that terrorise and
    control,
Avoiding the glances from drug dealers in case they need a
    messenger.

What can I give Him?
I am a refugee, all my possessions in my ragged bag,
Isolated, exhausted, rejected, unloved.
No sandals on my feet, no hope of a meal, of a kind word.
Moved on from border to border, a nuisance, a threat, a
    nobody.

What can I give Him?
My best pal blown up by an IED, the captain shot by rogue
    police,
My family far away, my daughter's first steps, my son bullied.
Sick of the heat, the dust, the suspicion, the lies,
I am so tired in this foreign land, yet clean my rifle for patrol.

What can I give Him?
Dressed in the customary red and white, a temporary job for
    the Season,
Made redundant after 40 years of loyalty.
Dishevelled is OK, I won't get employment anyway.
Why bother with interviews, only a few years till my bus pass.

What can I give Him?
Last few days for Amazon free delivery, which tablet does
    Sarah want?
Moet and Chandon for Jeremy, a Steiff bear for Emily.

Crowded streets and queues at tills, credit card refused;
I'll borrow from Wonga, think about the debt next year.

What can I give Him,
Poor as I am? —
If I were a Shepherd
I would bring a lamb;
If I were a Wise Man
I would do my part, —
Yet what I can I give Him, —
Give my heart.

*Note: First and last verse taken from 'A Christmas Carol'
poem by Christina Rossetti, published in 1872. More
familiarly known as the carol 'In the Bleak Midwinter'.*

Fishing in June

Father, I just thank you for the peace
And solitude here.
For the joy of being.
For success in catch
And being open to the elements
Of sparkling water, fresh breeze, rippling currents,
Azure sky and watery sun.
For the family of swans and numerous coots.
For the elegant tall bullrushes rising from their bed of straw
    leaves,
For the beauty of pearlescent fish.
For the freedom I have
To enjoy, explore, experience
More of You this year,
Even when I am not studying,
But just sharing the delights of Your world.
Thank you for kind people
Encouraging and helping me to learn and succeed
In fishing.

Fishing in January

Lord
It is cold and empty
I feel no reward
I cannot see clearly
Mist swirls around me and towards me
Chilling the temperature
The sky is opaque –
Your sunlight is not streaming through
Not even a glimmer
Or hope of warmth and radiance to come.
Nature pierces the frost yet bows to it
A touch aggravating the chill and extreme.
Closeted and snuggled in the warmth and protection of my
    clothes
My eyes cast down in introverted thinking
Fists clenched and toes curled
In the cold loneliness of despair and futility.
So much preparation and anticipation
For a heart of tears and self-blame.
Yet I press on to the next time.
Memories create a faith full hope for the future
Of promise and success and joy and excitement
Next time.

In the Rain

Father, you know when I am dry
When the sun beats down
No shade on my upturned leaves
I crack and wither
I droop and curl
I seek solace.
The surface is desert-dry and cracked
Under blistering heat.
I grasp moisture from the deepest depths
But there is no freshness there,
Its goodness diminished.

You see me, You notice me,
You come to me, You know what I need
You replenish me
Your life-giving cool water
Pours over me
The water splashes on my leaves
My thirst is quenched
My soul soil is soaked,
Absorbs the freshness
I am Wet. What joy!
Rejuvenated, drenched, cool,
Uplifted, sparkling, delighted.

You know me intimately

My innermost being
The needs of my soul
I am intimately known
And ultimately valued

Thank you that You know my name
And my care instructions.

Sitting Here in Silence
(on a Window Seat)

Cross-legged like a little pixie
Looking out on a sea of green from the Creator
Bathed in sunshine of the Son
Window slightly ajar
To feel the cool breeze of the Spirit
The rippling stream of life-giving water
Birdsongs of praise
Charismatic dancing and worship from the cow parsley
Soft gentleness of the blackbird perching on a
Wooden seat for rest
A book on Contemplative Prayer by my side
Grey shadows of trees and clouds
Patches of sunlight pass by
Ducks and chickens safely in their coop
No hurry here
Just sit in silence
Child, with Me.

Bluebells

The peace here is incredible
In the world but not involved in its busyness right now
Taking time
Just to enjoy my Creator's beautiful earth.
As traffic noises fade
All that surrounds me is birdsong,
The crackle of twigs,
The creaking of branches
And the whisper of rustling leaves.
No doubt ants are scurrying finding food
Birds are busying their nests
Hidden rabbits are burrowing,
But here in dappled warm sunlight
This glade is quiet, still and private.
No one knows I am here, only Jung[2] and God
And only we two know exactly.
It's been good to come off the path to a secluded place
I am here, Lord, amongst your bluebells,
Enveloped in waves of sapphire and denim, indigo and cobalt,
Heady within their fragrance.
Speak to me, Lord, for I am listening.

_____

[2] Jung is my husband

At Hell Bay, Bryher

God of power and might
How awesome are Your deeds.
Your love strong as the western sea
Pounding the shattered rocks
Incessant and strong.
You keep passionately loving
With a mighty strength
That doesn't give up
To unyielding rock,
But gradually they succumb
And crack and fall
To the power of Your Love.

Grief

A broken heart
Cracked, split
Not shattered into fragments
Still able to be connected
To fit again.
Sharp edges, revealing the grey inside
Rough and colourless.
The surface is smooth with
Comforting words, gold-painted hearts of hope.
But I live inside,
Revealed in my brokenness.
I see the three pieces
I hold them and fondle them in my hand.
I could place them together
But today I cannot do that.
I want to close my hand around one piece
To comfort it, to warm it,
But it causes me pain.
Do I have the courage to piece my broken heart together?
I can, but it is temporary.
It will take time to find the courage
To mend it properly, to place each part together
To ask the Holy Spirit for permanent fixative
But not today.

Note: As part of a retreat day, we were looking at the story of Ruth.

I found the intensity of the grief of Naomi very personally moving. She has lost her husband and both her sons and felt the Lord had turned His hand against her / dealt her a bitter blow.

On a table there was a basket of various hearts – we were asked to choose a heart and see what God was saying to us. I found three pieces of a broken heart and I was inspired to write this poem about Grief.

At Frensham Pond

Four beginners
Sailing in their brightly coloured dinghies
Cruising around the buoyed boundary
Returning frequently to base
Safe, secure, to discuss their journey.
Motored safety boat, watching, following,
Like a shark observing its prey,
Alert but aloof,
Aware but distant,
Letting them make their own mistakes.
Letting them learn, experiment, question, take action.
As the wind fills their sails
They soar across the blueness,
Uncontrolled speed from the elements.
But when against the wind
They battle to keep a straight path,
Tugging at the sails,
Pulling with all their might,
Acknowledging their weaknesses.

What a picture for me, Lord…
Help me to steer with the Wind
And enjoy the freedom of the cruise
But when hardships come,
To know that You can still the wind
Blowing in a different direction,

Causing me to rely on all You have taught me
And to trust through my learning
The skills You have gifted me
And the knowledge you have provided for me
Till I am confident in all winds
Stable, independent, fulfilled and content.
Amen.

A Father to a Father

I too lost my Son

An innocent life, well lived
Snatched by the snare of death
Too young, too sudden, too cruel
Overwhelming heartbreak, unbearable grief
Hopes unrealised, dreams unfulfilled
Empty answers to endless questions
Heavy silence instead of joyful laughter
Opaque clouds instead of sunlight

But I had power to raise My Son
The Authority to restore life
And I did so
Joy of re-engagement, uninterrupted unity, incessant love

I too raise your son
Into My arms
Know he is safe

One day you will meet again
For eternity
This is My promise
A Father to a father

(Love from your Father God)

At Whitehill Chase

So, Father,
I sit amongst the birdsong,
A smouldering autumn fire,
Cool air, scattering leaves.
The poignancy of the Cross.
The seat that beckons rest, solitude:
To meditate on Your Word,
To absorb your Holy Spirit,
To be thirsty,
To check my cleanliness,
To ask for more.
More fulfilling, more comfort, more enabling,
More gifts, more wisdom, more discernment.
To see the light shine in the darkness,
To see healings and new life.
To see Your Name lifted high in honour and praise.
The worldly traffic rumbles on in the background
Yet here now is the most beautiful of places to be,
Enveloped in the Kingdom here
With a Father who loves me.
Still, and at peace with life.
Thank you.

An Early Round Robin 2020

Round Robins will be rather short, what have I done this year?
Survived the lockdown, stayed at home – avoiding Covid fear.
Work was furloughed, home is cleaned, I went for local walks,
Home-schooled my kids and wore my mask, had social-
   distanced talks.
Clapped with neighbours, sanitised, protected NHS.
Couldn't hug my family, which caused me some distress.
Watched our Boris on TV, Professor Chris, Sir Pat,
Waited for my letters from health secretary Matt.
Saved lives by obeying all the updates on at five,
Placed soft toys in the window as Ocado vans passed by.
Zoomed in meetings, painted rainbows, cleared the loft and
   shed.
Comfort-eating handmade cakes, found books I hadn't read.
Cancelled trips (refunded most), and watching films till late
Stayed alert, abandoned beach, but garden's looking great.
No Mother's Day or Father's Day, nor Easter singing hymns
I only know it's Sunday cause I hear the church bells ring.
So goodbye, 2020, sing loudly Auld Land Syne
For old acquaintance I've forgot, it's been too long a time!

Similar Books by the Publisher

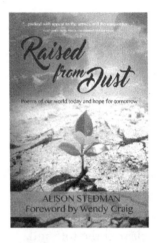

Raised from Dust
Alison Stedman

ISBN 978-1-911086-82-6

Through her poems, Alison takes us on a journey around the world, from the familiar sight of a homeless man on the streets to the wonders of Asian countryside and culture. With sentiments echoing Ecclesiastes, she mourns the transient nature of our lives, but then flips the coin and explores birth and rebirth, leading to an eternal hope.

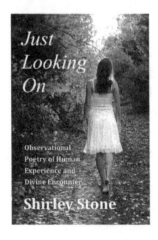

Just Looking On
Shirley Stone

ISBN 978-1-910197-08-0

Shirley Stone's illustrated poetry provides a fresh and vibrant approach to applying the truths found in Scripture to modern life and experience. Filled with priceless observations and insights about the world around us, each poem comes with a Bible verse and can be used as a daily meditation.

Books available from all good bookshops and from the publisher: **www.onwardsandupwards.org**